PowerHiking

SEATTLE

FOURTEEN
GREAT WALKS
THROUGH
THE STREETS OF SEATTLE
AND ENVIRONS

CAROLYN HANSEN   CATHLEEN PECK

Art direction and design	Dennis Gallagher and John Sullivan
	Visual Strategies, San Francisco [visdesign.com]
Maps	Kit Gallagher
Photography	Carolyn Hansen
	additional stock photos
Copy Editor	Elissa Rabellino
Printer	Overseas Printing Inc.
Publisher	PowerHiking Ltd.

Printed in China

PowerHiking

FOREWORD

Surrounded by the splendor of Puget Sound, the greenery of the Olympic and Cascade Mountains, and the sparkling water of Lake Washington, *Seattle* is a picturesque jewel of the Northwest. Fascinating history filled with intrigue and a mixing of cultures, along with industrial growth and innovation, combine to create an exciting atmosphere. Architecturally beautiful buildings rise downtown next to brick structures of the past, all situated near the iconic Space Needle. There are old fashioned streetcars, a modern monorail, and hidden staircases. Ferries ply the waters carrying people and cars to and from the Seattle waterfront and the many waterside neighborhoods. There are pleasure craft, fishing boats, large tankers, container ships, and the waterways are alive with people. Gardens and parks abound with glorious flowers and trees. Our exploration of this splendid city was eye opening as we delved into its amazing history and cultural influences. We were able to imagine life in *Seattle* in days gone by and enjoy it today. We hope that you will enjoy it too.

We measured our time and distances with a GPS device and diligently noted names of shops, restaurants and cafés that we visited. Some may change as businesses come and go. There may be slight variations as you do the hikes. Everyone walks at a different pace and will spend more time at certain areas of interest. *PowerHiking* makes it easy for you to explore as you wish, depending on your own agenda. Any discrepancies in the maps or directions are ours, and we hope you will forgive small inaccuracies.

We are particularly grateful to the ladies of the Sunset Club for their many spirited and thoughtful suggestions. Their ideas and help made our exploration of the enchanting neighborhoods so enjoyable. A special thank you goes to Sally Morbeck for her generosity as hostess and guide, and to Casey Carlson-Iffert who freely gave of her time and knowledge of the city. We are continually grateful to our power partners, John and Rodney. The creativity and talent of our design team, John Sullivan and Dennis Gallagher, continues to amaze us.

Carolyn Hansen, Cathleen Peck

THINGS TO KNOW BEFORE YOU GO

YOUR STYLE IN SEATTLE

Seattle can be damp and drizzly and there is frequent rain. The mornings can be foggy, cloudy and damp, sometimes clearing by mid-day and warming. You need to be prepared with a light hooded raincoat or a small packable umbrella and it is best to wear layers. If it is not drizzly and cloudy and the sun is out, the weather can be quite warm. A second pair of walking shoes is a good idea in case one pair gets wet. August generally has the best weather and is the most agreeable time to visit.

GETTING ABOUT THE CITY

Seattle has an excellent public transportation system. You can easily get about town on Metro Transit, the local bus line, free in the heart of downtown. There is the monorail, the light rail (from the airport to downtown), streetcars, water taxis, lake and bay cruises, and the Washington State Ferry. It is best to check online for schedules and location.

Seattle's Neighborhood Restaurants

SIGHTSEEING AND EVENTS

The Seattle City Pass is available online. You can save on entry fees to major attractions and, usually, there is a special line for those with the Pass. There is also the Go Seattle Card and the Go Select Pass. Information and purchase are available online and the cards are worth the cost as many tourist attractions are included.

Seafair is an annual citywide event occurring the first week of August. There is a triathlon, a torchlight decorated boat parade, and hydroplane races on Lake Washington. It coincides with Navy Fleet Week, with air shows by the Blue Angels. It is great fun with festivities throughout the city. Naval ships come into port and the lakes and waterways are filled with boats of Seattle residents as well as visiting boats.

SECURITY

Like in all urban centers, there are unfriendly neighborhoods. *Powerhiking Seattle* does not lead you into these neighborhoods. However, good advice for any city is to always be aware of your surroundings and keep close guard on your valuables.

RESTAURANTS AND FOOD

Seattle is a city full of wonderful restaurants and good food. While famous for seafood and waterside eateries, there are many fine choices in the various neighborhoods. Make every meal a special treat. You will not be without coffee as *Seattle* is the home to *Starbucks* and you will find one on almost every corner.

PowerHiking | SEATTLE

WHAT IS POWERHIKING?

PowerHiking is walking with an agenda that excites not only your senses but also your spirit. It takes walking to a new level of energy and interest and allows you to see and to do as much as possible. Your days are full of exhilarating experiences and exercise. *PowerHiking* permits you to see more of the unexpected – a spectacular view, a hidden staircase, a lakeside pathway, a magnificent old tree. In *Seattle*, *PowerHiking* takes on a whole new meaning. The stunning views of *Puget Sound*, snow covered *Mount Rainier*, the *Olympic Mountains*, *Lake Washington, Lake Union*, and the dazzling blue *Elliott Bay* are all there to be discovered. The city embodies the settlement of the northwest, from the original indigenous settlers, the fishermen, the gold rush fortune seekers, and the lumber barons. All – along with the more recent

influence of technological and air industry entrepreneurs – helped to create the *Seattle* we see today.

Although we spend very full days *PowerHiking* the richness that is *Seattle*, the walks can be divided into less strenuous excursions, with more time devoted to the pleasures of parks, lakesides, outdoor cafés, and ferry boat rides. You may choose to spend only a few hours exploring the city or follow the longer routes that take you through the many varying neighborhoods. The city is truly a feast to enjoy, as you prefer. You are in charge of your experience, and walking from one destination to the next is the key! Wear your *PowerHiking* shoes, take a bottle of water, a camera, and this book, and head out on your *Seattle PowerHike*!

CONTENTS

1

PIKE PLACE MARKET

- -

Pike Place Market

Victor Steinbrueck Park

Pike Place Hillclimb

Heritage Center

TIME All day | **DISTANCE** 2 miles

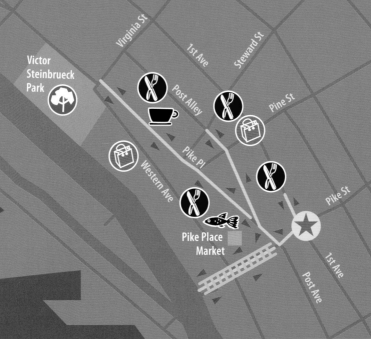

Victor
Steinbrueck
Park

Virginia St

1st Ave

Steward St

Post Alley

Pine St

Pike Pl

Western Ave

Pike St

Pike Place
Market

1st Ave

Post Ave

ELLIOTT BAY

One of the more eclectic and enjoyable attractions in *Seattle* is *Pike Place Market.* The market is unique and rich in history, from the early settlers to ongoing urban renewal. It is

referred to as "the soul" of *Seattle* and is the original farmers' market. Eight farmers started it over 100 years ago, in 1907. It has grown considerably, and not only is it

a major tourist attraction, but it is also where *Seattle* goes to shop. If you are looking for fresh fish, fresh fruit, flowers, baked goods

or crafts, you can find just about anything at **Pike Place Market**. There are charming restaurants and stores, apartments, as well as craft booths and street

performers lining the busy street in front. The market covers nine acres, and many historic buildings and fascinating stories are connected with the market and the vendors. As in the past, these purveyors grow the fruit they sell, catch the fish

fresh each morning, and butcher the meat themselves. Each visit to the market is an

exploration as you discover a new vendor,

taste something special, or enjoy a new

musician. From tea to spice to honey to

glass to clothes to pottery, it is all here

to enjoy. Everywhere you turn, there

is an explosion of flowers, vegetables,

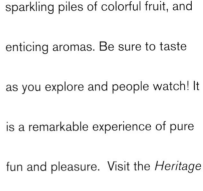

sparkling piles of colorful fruit, and enticing aromas. Be sure to taste as you explore and people watch! It is a remarkable experience of pure fun and pleasure. Visit the *Heritage Center* on *Western Avenue* to learn more historical facts about the market and its buildings. There are wonderful restaurants and bakeries and **Pike Place Market** is an excursion in itself. However, if you are short on time, this

PowerHike can be combined with the **Waterfront** or **Downtown Seattle** chapters.

We start our **PowerHike** at the corner of *1st Avenue* and *Pike Street*. Just down the cobblestones of *Pike Street* is the main entrance to the market. A few steps beyond the corner on *1st Street* is the *Crumpet Shop.* This cozy breakfast and luncheon spot offers homemade crumpets in a myriad of different

presentations. Watch the crumpets being made as you enjoy a treat. Walk back to *Pike Street* and down the cobblestone street to *Post Alley* and turn right.

Several interesting cafés and restaurants are located along this quaint alley—*Cafe Campagne, Post Alley Pizza, The Tasting Room, Kell's Irish Pub* and *The Pink Door*, a colorful little restaurant tucked away in an amazing old house with a beautiful terrace overlooking *Elliott Bay*. It has no sign and is, not surprisingly, behind a pink door. Any of these settings would be perfect for lunch or to return to later for dinner. Could it possibly be time to eat again? Through the arch and across *Pine Street,* is the flagship *Sur La Table* and, beyond, the *Inn at the Market*. This charming boutique hotel offers a superb northwest

experience. Walk past the chic boutique, *Fini*,

into the ivy covered patio and discover the

tranquility of its setting. There you will also find

Campagne and *Bacco Café,* both worthy of

a visit.

Retrace your steps along *Post Alley* to *Pike*

Street and go right, passing

the glorious fruit and vegetable

stands in the landmark Corner

Market Building, where the vendors are offering a taste of their delicious looking

produce. Upstairs is the *Pike Place Bar and Grill*, with extraordinary bay views. At

the corner of *Pike Place* turn right to wander down a street filled with amazing food

shops. It is a foodie's fantasy! One after another there are sandwich shops, fruit

stands, vegetable stands, a tea shop, Greek

food, and fresh salmon, which they will ship.

There are lines of people at each of these

shops. You will see *Beecher's Homemade*

Cheese, where

you can watch

the cheese being made in a huge tub in the window. A

taste is definitely in order. A little farther down is

The Confectional, a store with over 14 flavors

of cheesecake, decadent and made with pure

ingredients. There are large cheesecakes but also

mini cakes to taste and take with you. They ship and you can order online. Your nose

will lead you down the street to *Le Panier*, a French bakery, where not only is the

aroma amazing, but the croissants and sandwiches look delicious. It will be hard to

pass by and is a wonderful spot for breakfast or a snack. Just beyond is *Starbucks.*

This is the original store, and you will always find a line out the door. As you pass the original mermaid logo and go inside, you can indulge in a treat or souvenir. *Pike Market Coffee* is available – the only *Starbucks* where this special blend can be purchased – a great gift for your caffeinated friends! Back on the street, there is an ice cream shop and another deli or two. Once you are supplied with snacks, coffee and treats, cross the street at *Virginia Street* to *Victor Steinbrueck Park* for a moment of rest and indulgence while taking in spectacular views of *Elliott Bay.* This scenic park is named after the man largely responsible for preserving the existence of the market. Notice the large totems in the park. No doubt there will be a musician or mime or two to amuse you as well.

Return toward the market on *Western*

Avenue, passing among the many street merchants. These vendors rent their spaces by the day, so rarely will you see them in the same location twice. Once inside the market, you will pass colorful flower vendors on one side and craft booths on the other side. You will know when you have reached the main entrance to the market on *Pike Street* because you will encounter *Rachel the Pig. Rachel* is made of bronze and stands in front of *Pike Place Fish Company,* one of the most entertaining market vendors. Rows of fresh fish are stacked in front, and customers are amused by the tossing of the fish from one mongerer to another. It is the most fun and famous part of the market. Tourists linger, watching as the large fish

fly from hand to hand. Wander through the upper level of

food vendors and then make your way down the stairs to

other shops and outside to visit the lower level restaurants. The *Pike Place Hillclimb*

is a staircase leading to Down Under, the lower levels of the market, and down to the

waterfront.

Pike Place Market

is a fascinating and

fun-filled *PowerHike*. Even though you have nibbled your way through this enticing

experience, now it is time to select a comfortable place to sit, relax and ponder the

history of this amazing market while enjoying the bountiful views of *Seattle*.

Tours of the market are available for groups and advance reservations are required.

2

SEATTLE WATERFRONT

- -

Pioneer Square

Underground Tour

Smith Tower

Occidental Square

Waterfall Garden Park

Klondike Gold Rush National Historical Park

International District

The Waterfront

Seattle Aquarium

Olympic Sculpture Park

TIME All day | **DISTANCE** 7 miles

Denny Way

Warren Ave N

Western Ave

Olympic Sculpture Park

ELLIOTT BAY

Alaskan Way

Pike St

Seneca St

Aquarium

Pier 55

Alaskan Way

2nd Ave

1st Ave

Pioneer Square

Yesler Way

Occidental Square Waterfall Garden P

S Main St

S Jackson St

Occidental Ave S

INTERNATIO DISTRICT

Steeped in history and maritime

tradition, the *Seattle Waterfront*

is an exciting and diverse venue

to visit. It is lively, historic,

interesting and is the heart

and soul of the original city of

Seattle. With spectacular vistas

of *Elliott Bay* (the bay on which

Seattle was founded) and the

major shipping activity on the bay, this *PowerHike* is

a fun adventure that includes sites of *Seattle* history.

Its diverse exploration ranges from the settlers of

Seattle to the maritime industry to the dazzling array of sculpture in a bayside park.

The **PowerHike** starts in **Pioneer Square** at *Yesler Way* and *James Street*.

First built in 1853, **Pioneer Square** is the original downtown of **Seattle** and the city's birthplace. It is the center of historical **Seattle** and the city's development from the first store and hotel to the waterfront lumber mill. The cobblestones

and horse drawn carriages give you a taste of days gone by. Following the fire

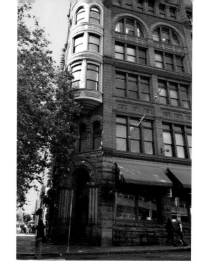

of 1889 that destroyed the wood buildings of the

first downtown, it was rebuilt with stone and brick, and many of the buildings remain

today. Once filled with brothels,

saloons, and gambling

halls, **Pioneer Square** exhibits the frontier history of the

city, as it was the jumping off point for the Klondike

Gold Rush in Alaska in 1897 and 1898. The wrought

iron pergola, a bust of Chief Seattle, and the tribal

totem pole were all added to the square in the early 1900s for the Alaska-Yukon-Pacific Exposition. The pergola was the cable car stop. It is a must to walk

under the pergola and into the *Seattle Historic Walkway*. A unique and "only in

Seattle" attraction is the unusual *Underground Tour*. Located at *Doc Maynard's*

Public House, a restored saloon located at *610 1st Street,* across from **Pioneer**

Square, the tour starts in this restored saloon and wanders through the old subterranean level of *Seattle*. It is an eye opening and fascinating view into historical stores and sidewalks of the past. After the fire, drainage issues caused buildings to be rebuilt at a higher level, but older, lower level entrances were retained. One can imagine the goings

on in the lower levels of early *Seattle*! *Pioneer Square* is where the term "skid row"

originated, as huge logs slid down *Yesler Street* to the mills on the waterfront. Look

up to the north of *Pioneer Square* to the *Smith Tower* at the corner of *Yesler Way*

and *2nd Avenue*. When it was completed in 1914, this beautiful building was the

tallest building west of the Mississippi

River. Take one of the original ornate brass

elevators to visit the observation deck for

a beautiful view of the city, the waterfront,

and the *Cascade* and *Olympic Mountains*.

Visit the *Chinese Room,* featuring antique Chinese

furniture.

Walk south on *1st Avenue* to *South Washington Street* and left to ***Occidental***

Square, a lovely tree lined plaza that is the location of shops, cafés, and galleries. On the first Thursday of each month there is an art walk, when all studios and galleries are open to visit. There are also four spectacular totem poles and the *Fallen Firefighters Memorial*. The square is always full of activity, particularly during the Fire Festival each July, and

you will most likely see musicians and mimes.

The nightclubs are quite lively in the evenings, but the neighborhood can be a bit rough, so it is best visited during the day. On the corner of *South Main Street* and

2nd Avenue, just through **Occidental Square**, is the

Waterfall Garden Park. Walk one block to 117 *South*

Main Street at the corner of *South Jackson Street* and

the **Klondike Gold Rush National Park**, a museum

dedicated to the Alaskan gold rush days.

If interest and time permit, follow *2nd Avenue*

to *South Jackson Street* and the beginning of

the **International District**. A visit to *Union*

Station and the famous *Panama Hotel* is a

treat. If not, turn right

and walk towards the

water on *South Jackson*

Street. At *1st Avenue,* turn right again, and you will find some interesting shops

filled with historical photos, native souvenirs, and local **Seattle** crafts. *Millstream* is

a particularly interesting shop for gifts from the

Pacific Northwest. There is also *The Original*

Drop Cookie, home of the famous original

Seattle cow chip cookie and worthy of stopping

in for a treat.

Return on *1st Avenue* to *Yesler Way* and turn left towards **Elliott Bay** and the

Alaskan Way. The **Seattle Waterfront** is

the heart of the city and, as you approach

the *Alaskan Way,* in front of you is the

Washington State Ferry Terminal at Pier 52.

Here is where you take the ferry to the outlying *Seattle* islands; and a little farther along at Pier 55 is *Argosy Cruises,* where you can catch a boat to *Blake Island* and the *Marine State Park* or *Tillicum Village*, or a harbor cruise around *Elliott Bay*. There is even a dinner cruise available. Turn right and walk the wide and lively walkway that follows the water along the piers. There are plenty of cafés, kiosks and restaurants to stop for refreshment. Not surprisingly, most feature seafood. *Ye Olde Curiosity Shop* at Pier 55 is worth a visit. It was first opened in 1899, and you will be amazed at the variety of *Seattle* souvenirs within its doors, as well as some delicious

homemade fudge. At Pier 57 is the

Waterfront Arcade, with its carousel,

and *Miners Landing*. The *Fisherman's*

Restaurant and Bar has interesting

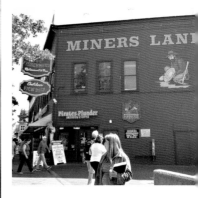

décor and an enticing deck on the water. Beyond

the park at Pier 59 is the *Seattle Aquarium*. There

are sea otters, jelly fish and a huge water dome – a

delight for all ages. The aquarium features the fish of

Puget Sound, and there is even a salmon hatchery

and fish ladder. Check the fish feeding schedule,

and visit the gift shop. Continue walking left along

the *Alaskan Way* as you exit the aquarium. Views over **Elliott Bay** are enchanting, and you may encounter a huge cruise ship docked for the day or, even possibly, a Navy cruiser near

the *Bell Street Conference Center* and *Anthony's Pier 66*,

with its delightful deck overlooking **Elliott Bay**. Across the

way is the *Marriott Waterfront Hotel,* with an appealing restaurant and patio, and just beyond the conference center

is the *Edgewater,* a charming hotel right on the water and with an

enticing restaurant, *Six Seven*. Continue walking towards the **Olympic**

Sculpture Park just beyond Pier 70 and above *Myrtle Edwards Park.* This is a

beautifully designed sculpture park with paths to wander, spectacular views, and

extraordinary outdoor sculptures. It is operated by the Seattle Art Museum, and the downtown green space was created from a contaminated brown field. After enjoying the *Olympic Sculpture Park,* retrace your steps along the *Alaskan Way*, stopping first at the *Waterfront Seafood Grill* at Pier 70, where the waters of

Elliott Bay lap against the outdoor deck. Here you can relax and enjoy the scenery

and boating sights of ***Elliott Bay,*** and be amazed at the influence of water on the

city of ***Seattle***. They will even provide you with

fleece blankets if the weather turns chilly. Relax and

reflect on all that you have seen in this diverse and

historic ***PowerHike*** into the beginnings of the city

of ***Seattle*** that we see today.

3

SEATTLE CENTER

- -

Space Needle

Experience Music Project

Science Fiction Museum
and Hall Of Fame

International Fountain

Kreielsheimer Promenade

Marion Oliver McCaw Hall

Phelps Center

Kobe Bell

Seattle Center House Theater

Key Arena

Northwest Craft Center and Gallery

Charlotte Martin Theater

Pacific Science Center

Fun Forest Pavillion and Rides

Monorail

Westlake Center

TIME All day | **DISTANCE** 3 miles

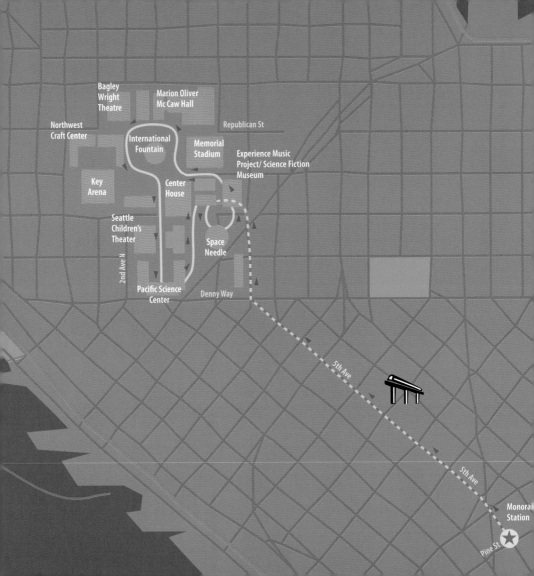

Bagley Wright Theatre

Marion Oliver Mc Caw Hall

Northwest Craft Center

Republican St

International Fountain

Memorial Stadium

Experience Music Project/ Science Fiction Museum

Key Arena

Center House

Seattle Children's Theater

Space Needle

2nd Ave N

Pacific Science Center

Denny Way

5th Ave

5th Ave

Monorail Station

Pine St

The **Space Needle**, iconic symbol of the city of **Seattle**, is the main attraction of

Seattle Center. Built for the World's Fair in 1962, **Seattle Center** was the futuristic

vision that is now the entertainment hub of

Seattle. It is the cultural center of the city

and a destination that the entire family can

enjoy. There is so much to see and do that

you will want to spend the better part of a

day exploring and enjoying the experience.

A monorail was built for the World's Fair

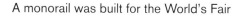

in 1962, and it is the best way to visit the **Space Needle**. Take the monorail from

Westlake Center on *Pine Street* for a three minute ride, and gaze at the view of the

Space Needle as you approach the station. Since it was built, **Seattle Center** has

changed and modernized with the addition of the *Experience Music Project (EMP)*, envisioned by Microsoft co-founder Paul Allen as a memorial to Jimi Hendrix, the celebrated **Seattle** rock star. The *EMP* architect is Frank Gehry, and the building is outrageously flamboyant. There is a collection of Hendrix guitars and the changing sound and light show is exciting. The *Science Fiction Museum and Hall of Fame*, with displays of artifacts from popular science fiction films and television shows, is also in the *EMP*. Adjoining these

visually exciting attractions is a beautifully designed cultural park with venues for

theater, ballet, and sports. In the middle is the *International Fountain* with dancing

water, as well as music and light displays. It is a beautiful, restful spot to balance the

stimulation of the other interactive entertainment.

We start the **PowerHike** at the monorail station

at *Westlake Center*. Buy a round-trip ticket and

enjoy the short ride into **Seattle Center**. As you

gaze at the spectacular site of the **Space Needle**, the excitement of the visit intensifies. It is the symbol of **Seattle** – a soaring testimony to innovation. Visit the *Observation Deck*, the *Space Base* gift shop, or the *Sky City Restaurant*.

Purchase the appropriate ticket and enjoy. The lines to the top can be long and there is a separate line for the restaurant. The *Observation Deck* offers unparalleled views of the city, *Puget Sound, Mount Rainier, Elliott Bay, Lake Union* and even *Safeco*

Field, home of the Seattle

Mariners baseball team. There

are telescopes (Swarovski!)

for closer views and you will

definitely want your camera!

User friendly maps describe

the sights from this incredible

location. If you are dining

at the *Sky City Restaurant*,

reservations are a must and

the line can be long. Worth

the wait, the restaurant

revolves 360 degrees as you enjoy your meal and the panoramic view. The *Skyline*

Level is available for private events. At *Space Base* you can purchase a unique

memento of the **Space Needle**. Open year round, a visit here is a **Seattle** must-do!

From the **Space Needle,** walk to

the right to visit the **Experience**

Music Project/Science Fiction

Museum. Enjoy the cavernous

entry hall free of charge, with its ever-changing soundtrack and light show. There is a charge to visit the other exhibits, but definitely worth your time if you are a fan of rock and roll. The gift shop has something fabulous for every fan. Walk into the

adjoining *Science Fiction Museum and Hall of Fame*. This is a unique exhibit, with its own gift shop, that will delight aficionados of science fiction as well as just the curious.

Upon leaving the fantasy environment, walk through

Center Square towards the

International Fountain.

Originally built for the

World's Fair, the fountain has

been modernized and now

is a place where children

play and the water is recycled. It is a favorite

spot in which to relax and enjoy the continuing

light and water show. Follow the *Kreielsheimer*

Promenade, passing *Memorial Stadium* to *Marion*

Oliver McCaw Hall, home to the Seattle Opera

and Ballet. Its beautiful glass façade welcomes

all through the *Grand Lobby* to the *Susan Brotman Auditorium*, the lecture halls, the *Prelude Café*, and *Amusements* gift shop. Adjacent to the left along *August Wilson Way* is *Phelps Center,* home of the Seattle Ballet, and *Bagley Wright Theater,* with its three Seattle repertory theaters. Continue on to *Kobe Bell*, and left to the *Seattle Center House Theater*, with its intimate design for concerts and family events. Just beyond is *Key Arena* where sports of all kinds

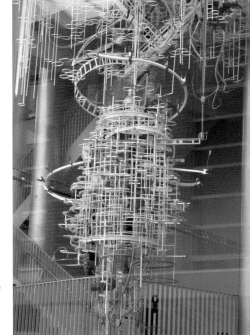

49

can be enjoyed. *Seattle*

Center is a convenient,

well designed home for

the city's performing arts.

As you pass the beautiful

fountains and blossoming

trees and just before *Key Arena,* visit the *Northwest Craft Center and Gallery,* featuring crafts from the Pacific Northwest - open daily except Monday. Walk past the fountain, jogging left and passing the *Charlotte Martin Theater* to the *Pacific Science Center*, an enormous and very popular destination,

with its many science exhibits. *Center House*, next to the monorail station, has a food court and is popular for its Children's Museum. If you are looking for a quiet and peaceful spot in which to rest and reflect, walk across the path and into the gardens. Once restored, you can experience the *Fun Forest Pavilion and Rides* next to the monorail station.

When you have enjoyed the amazing entertainment opportunities and cultural offerings **Seattle Center**

presents to its residents and visitors, walk back to the monorail for the return to *Westlake*

Center. Take advantage of the abundant shopping, or you can visit the food mall for a snack. There are many restaurants nearby, such as PF Chang's, Wild Ginger, and Palomino. There is also *Pike Place Market*, (explored in another chapter) with its plentiful food opportunities and choices, only a short walk away.

4 WASHINGTON PARK ARBORETUM

- -

Arboretum

Graham Visitor Center

Foster Island

Marsh Island

Lake Washington

University of Washington Football Stadium

Azalea Way

Rhododendron Glen

Japanese Garden

TIME 4–5 hours | **DISTANCE** 4–4.5 miles

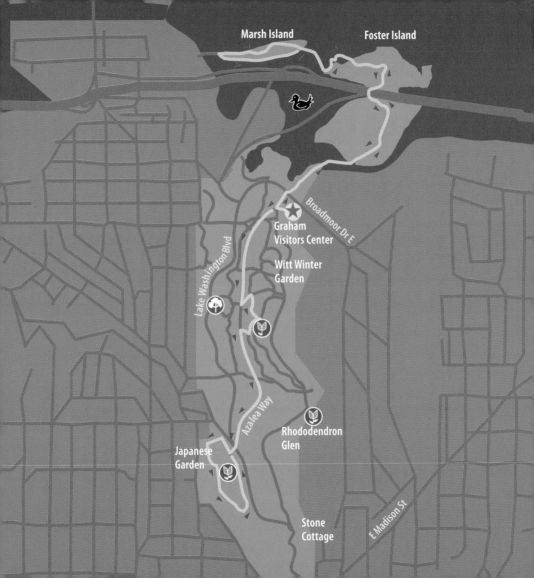

Marsh Island

Foster Island

Broadmoor Dr E

Graham
Visitors Center

Witt Winter
Garden

Lake Washington Blvd

Azalea Way

Rhododendron
Glen

Japanese
Garden

E Madison St

Stone
Cottage

In the idyllic setting of the

northwest, the beauty of

Seattle is dazzling. With

Mount Rainier in the

background, *Puget Sound*

in the foreground, *Lake*

Washington in front of you, and trees and greenery

surrounding you, the *Seattle* locale is breathtaking

to visit. ***The Washington Park Arboretum***,

on the shores of *Lake Washington,* displays

this magnificent grandeur, and an exploration of

this local treasure is a must when in *Seattle*. Featuring a vast array of native trees

and plants, the scenery is stunning in any season, and the ***Arboretum*** is truly

a horticultural adventure. Created in 1934, it has a vibrant assortment of native

trees and plants. There are 230 acres of

giant sequoias, meadows, enormous lawns,

magnificent rhododendrons, and native birds.

The park is jointly cared for by the city of **Seattle** and the University of Washington. The array of specially planted gardens includes the *Pacific Connections, Witt Winter* (a brief walk up the Hillside Trail), *Shoreline* (a wetland of fish and wildlife habitat) and *Japanese.*

This exciting **PowerHike** of **The Washington Park Arboretum** begins on *Arboretum Drive East* at the *Graham Visitor Center and Gift Shop*. Here you can arrange for a guided tour, find area maps, or select an audio tour. The gift shop at the *Visitor Center* is well worth a visit to find a distinctive selection of gifts for the home and garden or the shop specialty, bookmarks and

cards of pressed flowers.

One can circle the entire **Arboretum** from the

Visitor Center by following *East Arboretum*

Road to the left to *East Interlaken Blvd.*, going

right to *Lake Washington Blvd.* and right to

East Foster Island Blvd., where you can walk

to the lakeside trail. A right turn on *Arboretum*

Drive East brings you back to the *Visitor Center*. There are many paths and trails throughout the **Arboretum**, and they will all lure you to follow them and explore

through the picturesque array of trees and plants. The **Arboretum** is a haven to joggers, walkers and people strolling and enjoying this tantalizing **Seattle** treasure. The **PowerHike** of the **Arboretum**

is in two segments. We first walk to **Foster Island** and then **Marsh Island** through

the wonderful marsh area along the shores of **Lake Washington**. Leaving the *Visitor*

Center, cross *Arboretum Drive East* and follow the signs toward *The Marsh Trail*

straight ahead. Walking along, you will notice

a change in the greenery as the trees turn

to native marsh plants, such as cattails and

waterlilies, and will see myriads of ducks,

herons, and geese in *Duck Bay*.

Sparrows and goldfinches fly

about and sock-eye salmon

and cutthroat trout swim below.

As you emerge from the reeds

you will see the boardwalk trail

weaving through the shallows of

Lake Washington. Both **Foster**

Island and **Marsh Island** are a

result of draining water from the lake when the *Evergreen Floating Bridge* was built. Follow the boardwalk onto **Foster Island** as you enjoy the amazing views of the University of Washington football stadium across the water – almost close enough to touch. This part of the **Washington Park Arboretum *PowerHike*** is a marvelous opportunity to explore **Lake Washington** and the many birds that call it home. *The Marsh Trail* is a short 2 mile walk with many spots for resting, viewing or even a picnic or quiet time. Return along the boardwalk to the trail and the *Visitor Center* and follow *Azalea Way* through the middle of the **Arboretum** and the second part of the ***PowerHike***.

Head west from the *Visitor Center* toward *Azalea Way*. Astonishingly beautiful in the spring, this path is filled with azaleas, flowering cherry trees, rhododendrons, camellias, and dogwood trees. There are native birds throughout the **Arboretum**

so be sure to carefully watch and listen for them. Do not miss the *Witt Winter Garden*, featuring winter flowers and glorious dogwood and witch hazel trees. Do look for the ever-present hummingbirds. Visit *Rhododendron Glen*, with its vast collection of luscious rhododendrons. What an enchanting 1.5 mile walk!

As you reach *Lake Washington Blvd. East*, you come to the **Japanese Garden**. There is an admission fee but this splendid

garden is well worth a visit and there are free tours at varying times during the week. An array of magnificent Japanese maple trees as well as authentic landscaping and stone bridges lend to the serenity of this beautiful setting. In

the springtime, colorful azaleas hug the pathways and ponds and in the fall, the maples

put forth delirious color. Visit *Arbor of the Murmuring Pines Teahouse* and, with

reservations, a tea ceremony and the art of *chado.*

It has been an adventurous and beautiful **PowerHike**. Pick a favorite café or restaurant

to relax in and reflect on the glories of nature that you have experienced today.

(Note: This part of the **PowerHike** can be walked in reverse, parking at the

Japanese Garden and walking up the *Azalea Way* to the *Visitor Center, The Marsh*

Trail, and returning to the **Japanese Garden**.)

5 MADRONA

- - - - - - - - - -

TIME 3 hours | **DISTANCE** 2 miles

On the edge of a hilltop overlooking *Lake Washington*, *Madrona* is an excellent example of an old-time *Seattle* neighborhood, with beautiful gardens and trees and some of the area's most architecturally interesting homes. Filled with seasonal flowers, this *PowerHike* takes you through the charming neighborhood, its shopping lanes, and through picturesque *Madrona Woods Park*. There are enchanting stairways and paths through striking trees and exquisite

flowering bushes. This is a fairly short

PowerHike, and there is plenty of time

for brunch, lunch, or dinner at one of the

neighborhood restaurants. Delightful during

the weekdays, *Madrona* is a hot spot on

the weekends when everyone comes for

brunch.

We start on *Lake Washington Blvd.*

at *Madrona Park*. On the shores

of *Lake Washington*, *Madrona*

Park has picnic areas and lovely

swimming with a grassy beach, not

to mention glorious lake vistas. *Madrona Woods,* a

part of the park, is 9.2 acres of lush madrona trees

nestled on the hillside above the lake and across

Lake Washington Blvd. Madrona Park Creek, spring

fed, flows through the park. There are fish steps so it is possible to see salmon in

the creek. Bordered by native plants and stairways to the *Madrona* neighborhood,

Madrona Woods is a perfect start to exploring **Madrona.** After enjoying the park

and its lovely beaches, walk up the stairway at *East*

Marion Street and *38th Avenue*. It continues up to

35th Avenue, but you can also go right at *37th Avenue* to *Randolph Avenue* to the stairs going up *East Spring Street.*

Continue up to *34th Street,* which is the main street of the neighborhood. Wander on both sides of *34th Street,* exploring from *Marion*

Street to *East Pine Street* and

enjoying the distinctive shops such

as *décor on 34th*, galleries and

restaurants. There is

a tempting bakery,

VeriteCoffee and

Cupcake Royale,

and some delicious

restaurants, such

as *St. Clouds Food*

& Spirits and *Café*

Soleil. One particularly popular restaurant is in an

old Victorian-style house, the *HiSpot Cafe*. This trendy eatery has a lovely patio, a treat in warm weather, and it is best to make a reservation. Around the corner at *3406*

East Union Street is *Glassbaby*. The unique studio features hand blown votive candleholders in an amazing choice of colors. You can watch the glass blowers working in the back,

except during their lunch break. The shop was founded by a three-time cancer survivor, and a percentage of profits from some votives goes to various cancer centers. The glass votives come in a myriad of colors, and are very popular gifts. The shop will ship, so you do not have to carry them on your *PowerHike*. What a beautiful and meaningful souvenir of *PowerHiking Seattle*.

After visiting *Glassybaby*, begin the *PowerHike* back down to *Madrona Park* on *Lake Washington*. Take the stairs down *Union Street* to *37th Street,* then right following *Randolph Avenue* to *East Marion Street* and left down the steps, admiring

the vintage homes, lovely gardens, and magnificent trees that make **Madrona** such

a special neighborhood. Cross *Lake Washington Blvd.* to the park and relax, gazing

over the lake to *Mount Rainier*. *PowerHiking* takes you to the most beautiful places!

Note: You can take the MT2 bus to 34th Street in Madrona from downtown.

6

HIRAM M. CHITTENDEN LOCKS
DISCOVERY PARK
BALLARD

- -

Puget Sound Lake Washington Ship Canal

Visitor Center

Carl S. English Jr. Botanical Garden

Large And Small Locks

Fish Ladder

Commodore Park

Discovery Park

Daybreak Star Indian Cultural Center

Ballard Avenue N.W. Shops and Cafés

TIME 4–5 hours | **DISTANCE** Chittenden Locks–2 miles;

Discovery Park–2 miles; Ballard–2 miles

Chittenden Locks

NW 54th St

30th Ave NW

Carl S. English Jr.
Botanical Garden

Visitor Center

Hiram M. Chittenden Locks

Administration
Building

Commodore
Park

Fish Ladder

W Commodore Way

SALMON BAY

Ballard

24th Ave NW

NW 58th St
NW 57th St
NW 56th St

NW Market St

Tallman Ave NW
Russell Ave NW
Leary Ave NW
Ballard Ave NW
Shilshole Ave NW

Ballard Terminal RR

W Commodore Way

Ray's
Boathouse

37th Ave NW

34th Ave NW

30th Ave NW

24th Ave NW

Shilshole

39th Ave W

42nd Ave W

47th Ave W

Seaview Ave NW

SALMON BAY WATERWAY

NW Market St

NW 54th St

Ballard Terminal R R

Daybreak
Star Indian
Cultural Center

W Cramer St

Discovery Park

W Lawton St

Hiram M.
Chittenden Locks

Commodore
Park

Utah Ave

Texas Way

36th Ave W

34th Ave W

W Harley St

W Fort St

W Commodore

Gilman Ave W

Forming part of the *Seattle Lake Washington Ship Canal*, the **Hiram M. Chittenden Locks**, built in 1911, are a fascinating landmark and unique to the city of **Seattle.** Developed by engineer, Hiram

M. Chittenden, from shallow canals used for floating logs, the locks today are an

important engineering project designed to protect the **Seattle** freshwater lake system from the saltwater of *Puget Sound* while permitting passage of vessels of all sizes. They are a not-to-be-missed part of the **Seattle** lifestyle. The locks move boats from the fresh water level of *Lake Washington*

and *Lake Union* to the salt water level of *Puget Sound.* Handling both pleasure and commercial boats, the two locks are an integral part of the **Seattle** waterways and mesmerizing to observe. Boats and ocean going vessels enter at one level, and the locks fill or release water – depending on the direction – so that the boat can move on. The museum has an exhibit explaining how the system works. The locks also have a fish ladder with an underground

viewing area – fascinating! The salmon enter the ladder from the salt water *Shilshole Bay* and then jump up the levels to enter the fresh water of *Salmon Bay* on their way to the lake or stream of their birth. At that point, they spawn and die shortly after.

We start at the *North*

Entry to the locks off *NW*

54th Street. Walk through

the beautiful gates and

down the flower lined

path to the *Visitor Center.*

In the *Visitor Center,* the *Northwest Gift Shop*

has information and souvenirs, and there are

brochures and books explaining the locks. The

upstairs museum has a wonderful historical

exhibit as well as a visual and hands-on exhibit

of how the locks operate. Start with the film

Enjoy a stroll through the
Carl S. English Jr. Botanical Garden

In front of you is a world renowned garden with over 500 plant species. Please help protect our rare and unique plants by not picking flowers, climbing the trees, or walking in the plant beds. Enjoy a variety of wildlife in the garden. For your safety and their well-being, please do not feed, chase or pet the wildlife.

Visitor Center and Gift Shop
For more information, please stop in our visitor center just ahead on the left. Restrooms, water, a gift shop and exhibits are available here.

Did You Know?
Western spring beauty, *Claytonia sibirica*, is one of these plant species discovered by Carl English. Look for pinkish stripes on the petals of this flower. These stripes help attract insect pollinators. Think of the stripes like runway lights for airplanes. Tiny insects, land over here!

explaining the history and function of the locks. Winter and summer hours of the *Visitor Center* vary, so it is best to check the web site before visiting. There are free guided tours of the locks, fish ladder, and botanical garden at various times during the day. The locks themselves are open year round from 7 AM to 9 PM.

From the *Visitor Center,* walk left on the main pathway to the garden path. Walk right and follow the pathway in a circle through the *Carl S. English Jr. Botanical Garden*. English, who designed the garden in 1931, brought in many specimens of trees and

flowers to create the beautiful
English style garden you see
today. Breathtaking to enjoy, it
hosts concerts at various times
during the year.

Complete the garden pathway
circle and return to the main path,
PowerHiking to the right passing
the Administration Building and
surrounding rose gardens to the
locks. The first lock is the *Large
Lock* and beyond it, the *Small*

Lock. Walkways cross the locks,

closing when vessels pass through.

From canoes to ferry boats to barges

to fishing boats to passenger ships,

the locks permit them to pass from

Puget Sound to *Salmon Bay* by

raising the water level 26 feet, or

by lowering it the same amount for

boats going in the opposite direction.

People stand for hours watching the

boats go up and down and back and

forth. It is truly remarkable!

Cross the *Small Lock* walkway and the walkway

between *Salmon Bay* and *Shilshole Bay* to

the *Fish Ladder*. One of few fish ladders where

freshwater and salt water meet, the 21 step

ladder was built in 1976 to replace the existing

10 step ladder built in 1916. The viewing

gallery, with its large windows, permits viewers

to watch as the salmon struggle to return

to their spawning grounds and continue the

cycle honored

by Northwest

Indians for

hundreds of years. There are tours and interactive displays explaining the life cycle of the salmon. To enable visitors to experience traveling through the locks, Argosy

Cruises has a lock cruise departing from Pier 56 through *Elliott Bay* to the locks and through the

locks to *Lake Union*. It lasts two hours and is part of the City

Pass and Go Card Seattle.

If you only have time for a short **PowerHike**, you can

retrace your steps back across the lock

pathways and finish back at the entrance.

However, this *PowerHike* continues on

–*PowerHiking* through *Commodore*

Park, with its beautiful vistas of the

ship canal, and up *West Commodore*

Way toward **Discovery Park.** At *40th*

Avenue West, continue uphill, turning

right to *Texas Street* and into the park.

This is **Seattle's** largest park, with almost

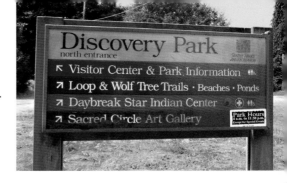

12 miles of trails. Located on Magnolia Bluff, there are forest groves, incredible

views, secluded beaches, sand dunes, meadows, fabulous old trees, wildlife, and

a lighthouse. **Discovery Park** was once Fort Lawton, a

prisoner-of-war camp during the Civil War. There is a visitor

center and a historic section with wonderful colonial buildings

– something for everyone's interest and an area where one

could spend hours exploring and enjoying. You

can choose the *Loop Trail* (2.8 miles), any number

of short trails, or the *Beach Trail* (a 2 mile trip).

We follow *Beach Trail* towards the arts center and

the *Daybreak Star Indian Cultural Center.* Be sure to

marvel at the view and reflect a bit (or picnic) on one

of the benches on the *North Bluff* overlooking *Puget*

Sound. The *West Point Lighthouse* is down below,

and the reflecting ponds are to the right. Follow the

trail back to *Texas Street,* turning left down the hill and

right onto *West Commodore Way,* returning to the

Hiram M. Chittenden Locks.

A short ride along *NW Market Street*

off *NW 54th Street* leads you to

Ray's Boathouse, on the left at

6049 Seaview Avenue NW. With a

constantly changing fresh seasonal

menu, **Ray's Boathouse** is popular

with locals and tourists alike. The

spectacular setting on the bay lends

itself to relaxed dining, boat watching, and stunning views of *Puget Sound* and the *Olympic Mountains*. It is not to be missed and a perfect spot to relax following your tour of the **Hiram M. Chittenden Locks.**

Return on *NW Market Street* to *24th Avenue* and the neighborhood of **Ballard**. Formerly a fishing village with Scandinavian heritage, **Ballard** is now the home of popular bars and restaurants. The *Majestic Bay Theater* has been recently restored and is the oldest operating movie theater in the country. Turn onto *Ballard*

Avenue NW and walk both sides of this historic street, enjoying the chic shops and enticing cafés. The bell tower in

the small central park has the original bell from **Ballard's** city hall, built in 1899, that stood where the bell tower is today. Choose one of the friendly local spots in this diverse **Seattle** neighborhood and relax and enjoy a thoughtful time of all that you have seen and enjoyed in the **PowerHike**.

7

MADISON PARK
MADISON VALLEY

- - - - - - - - - - - - - - - - - -

Madison Park

Lake Washington

Samuel Hyde House

Madison Park Village

TIME 3 hours | **DISTANCE** 1 mile

Mad
Park

Samuel Hyde
House

Washington Park
Arboretum

Azalea Way E

Arboretum Dr E

Lake Washington Blvd E

E Madison St

MADISON VALLEY

LAKE WASHINGTON

29th Av E

On the shores of *Lake Washington* and beyond the *Washington Park Arboretum* is the quaint village of **Madison Park**. Originally this was a popular destination of

lakeside summer homes. Now it is an upscale neighborhood of swank houses and gated gardens and a favorite recreational spot. On the *Puget Sound* side of the Arboretum is the neighborhood of **Madison Valley**. We explore the chic shops and well known French restaurants of **Madison Valley**, and the lovely lakeside vistas, boutiques, restaurants, and cafés of **Madison Park**.

Start this **PowerHike** at the corner of *Lake Washington Blvd. East* and *East Madison Street*, just beyond the entrance to the **Washington Park Arboretum**. *East Madison Street* stretches from the shores of *Puget Sound* all the way across the city of **Seattle** to the shore of *Lake Washington,* and was named after President James Madison. It was designed by John McGilvra, original owner of much of the land in the **Madison Park/Madison Valley** area. Walk to the right on *East Madison Street* into the intriguing neighborhood of **Madison Valley**. Once hunting and fishing land of the Duwamish Indians, the neighborhood now is filled with parks and charming homes. Stretching all the way to *23rd Avenue East,* we explore just a small area of this dynamic neighborhood that circles part of the *Arboretum.* Two blocks down we

come to *Lavender Heart,* a delightful

boutique. It is worth a visit inside to

marvel at the amazing variety of items, not

to mention soaps! In the patio just before

reaching *Lavender Heart* is *Rover's,* the famous French

restaurant of the Chef in the Hat, Thierry Rautureau. Originally

from France, **Seattle's** famous chef is always seen

wearing a fedora, thus his nickname. On the corner

is his newest café and neighborhood spot, *Luc,* and

across the street is the French bistrot *Voilà!* Walk left

in the direction of *Lake Washington* less than half a

mile to this **PowerHike's** next destination, **Madison**

Park and the village of this attractive neighborhood. As

we walk toward **Madison Park**, we explore the cafés and

shops along the way. At *38th Street*

is the *Samuel Hyde House,* part

of the National Register of Historic

Places. Built in the early 1900s by

liquor tycoon Samuel Hyde, this stately

brick colonnaded mansion is now the

Russian Consulate. Continue on to the

charming lakeside village, visiting all of the inviting shops

along the way. Be sure to visit *Martha E. Harris.* It will be

difficult not to indulge in a souvenir in this enticing and much

loved shop. At the foot

of *East Madison Street*

at *Lake Washington*

is **Madison Park.**

Walk through this lovely grassy park and onto the path by the lake, a perfect spot to take in the magnificent vista as well as view the *Evergreen Point Floating Bridge.* You will also see *Pioneer Hall,* a historic early 1900s brick building that is the meeting location for Pioneer Association of the State of Washington, an

organization dating from the pioneer days.

After enjoying the breathtaking scenery, retrace your steps

back through the village and to one of the many tempting

cafés or restaurants that you have passed. Whether it

is the cozy fire at *Red Onion, Cactus, Madison Park*

Café, Attic Ale House and Eatery, McGilvra's, or *Bing's*

Bar & Grill for one of their bodacious burgers, relax and

enjoy this quite beautiful

Seattle PowerHike.

8   DOWNTOWN SEATTLE

- - - - - - - - - - - - - - - - - - - -

Pike Place Market

1st Street Stores

Seattle Art Museum (SAM)

The Harbor Steps

Hammering Man

Benaroya Hall

Garden of Remembrance

Central Library

Westlake Center

Nordstrom Flagship Store

Pacific Place

TIME 3–4 hours | **DISTANCE** 3 miles

(depending on time spent in the museum)

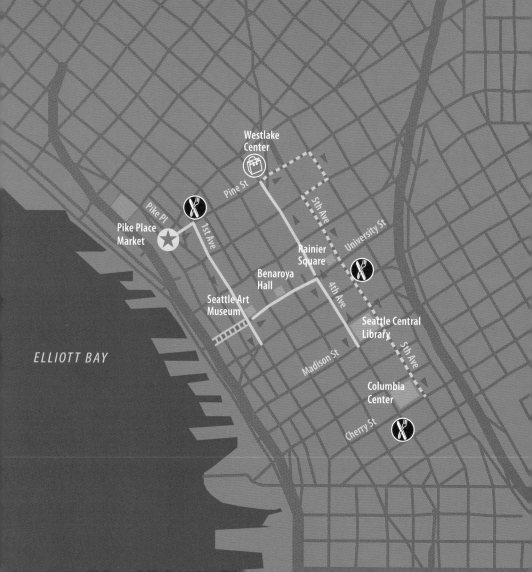

ELLIOTT BAY

Pike Place Market

Pike Pl

1st Ave

Westlake Center

Pine St

5th Ave

University St

Rainier Square

Benaroya Hall

4th Ave

Seattle Art Museum

Madison St

Seattle Central Library

5th Ave

Columbia Center

Cherry St

The heart of **Downtown Seattle** is the perfect **PowerHike**. It is a compact location with something for everyone, including fine stores, fascinating small shops, galleries, a world-

class art museum, a beautiful concert hall, and an architecturally intriguing **Central Library**. We walk uphill and downhill, necessary after feasting at **Pike Place Market**. On every block is a *Starbucks* so you never run out of caffeine-generated energy. **Seattle** runs on coffee! Bordered by **Pike Place Market, Seattle City Center**, and **Pioneer Square**, **Downtown Seattle** is a highlight of the city.

We start at the corner of *Pike Place* and *Pine Street*. Visit one of the many eateries at **Pike Place Market** or the original *Starbucks,* and walk uphill on *Pine Street* in the direction of *1st Avenue*. On the left is *The Inn at the Market*, with restaurants and the *Fini* boutique. Peek inside and then continue up to *1st Avenue* and turn right. Many intriguing shops line the street, including *The Crumpet Shop*, where crumpets in all varieties are made to order in front of you. It is definitely worth a stop. Continue to the corner of *University Street*, passing *Union Street* and

the beautiful *Four Seasons Hotel,* where you encounter one of **Seattle's** favorite

shops, *Fran's Chocolates.* You will find

extraordinary and luscious creations

for a yummy treat or beautifully boxed

chocolates for gifts. At *University Street*

is the **Seattle Art Museum**. The *Harbor*

Steps are just across *1st Avenue –*

a lovely place to sit and enjoy the view of

Elliott Bay and gaze across at the 48

foot moving sculpture, *Hammering Man,*

in front of the internationally celebrated

museum. Made out of steel and aluminum

and designed by Jonathan Borofsky,

Hammering Man is one of several similar

sculptures throughout the world. Inside the

main entrance of the *Seattle Art Museum*,

you are greeted with the kinetic sculpture

of suspended white cars, *Inopportune: Stage One*. Once in the galleries, you will

be enthralled with the Northwest Coast Indian art among the many other unique exhibits. The galleries are spacious and well-lighted, and it is pure pleasure to visit. On the lower level, a marvelous gift shop carries art books and unique works from local artists. The museum opens at 10AM and is closed Mondays, Tuesdays, and most major holidays.

Upon leaving the museum, turn left and walk one block on *1st Street* to *Ancient Grounds*, a unique coffeehouse and art shop specializing in Northwest Indian and African art, among other treasures. The coffee is good, too. There is also the enchanting shop, *de Medici Ming Fine Paper*, with beautiful greeting cards and

wrapping papers from around the world. Back at the corner of *University Street* turn uphill to *3rd Avenue* and **Benaroya Hall**, the home of the Seattle Symphony Orchestra. With two performing halls, the symphony hall has state-of-the-art acoustics, and a Chihuly sculpture consisting of two chandeliers, *Crystal Cascade*, to enjoy. Other works of art are also in and around the symphony hall, and tours are available on Tuesday and Friday at noon and 1PM. Inside are a gift shop, a café, a dining room for pre-concert dinner, and, of course, *Starbucks*. Outside is the serene *Garden of Remembrance*, a memorial to residents of

Washington State killed in conflicts

since World War II.

Continue up *University Street* and

turn right on *4th Avenue*, passing

the *W Hotel* on the way to the

architecturally surprising **Central**

Library, between *Spring Street* and *Madison Street.* (You may like to take a quick peek inside the W to admire the lobby décor.) The library is a unique and striking building. Constructed in 2004, it received LEED Silver status for its environmental sophistication. It was designed to be multi-media, and there is room for 400 computers for public use. Much of the space is designed for the comfort of the users, including a mini-café for a quick beverage or snack just next to a study area. It is worth exploring the interior and going up to the top floor. The views are wonderful, and the extraordinary natural light that emanates from the mesh exterior is pleasing.

Architectural tours are available, and you

should inquire about the times at the main

desk on the first floor.

Downtown Seattle has many popular

restaurants. There is *McCormick's Fish House*

and Bar just two blocks beyond the **Central**

Library on *4th Avenue* at *Columbia Street.*

Wild Ginger is at *3rd Avenue*

and *Union Street. Rock Bottom*

is at *Rainier Square,* 5th

Avenue and *University Street.*

Wherever you choose, it will

be a treat. Continue on to the many exciting shops downtown. Go left on *4th Avenue* to *Pine Street* and the **Westlake Center**, home to many specialty shops and dining establishments, including the *Washington State Shop,* with native and Washington State made items as well as smoked salmon and other Washington delicacies. Across the street on the corner of *5th Avenue* and *Pine Street*

is the *Nordstrom* flagship store. At *6th Avenue* and *Pine Street* is **Pacific Place**, a complex offering more shopping, dining and entertainment. On *6th Avenue* is

Mario's, a boutique exclusive to the Northwest, offering men's and women's designer clothing and accessories. It is a beautifully designed store and worth a visit.

This is a perfect location to end the **PowerHike**, but there is one more destination worth the walk to visit. Follow *5th Street* nine blocks to *Cherry Street* and the **Columbia Center**. It is currently

Seattle's tallest building, 1,049 feet above sea level. Go up to the Observation

Deck. The view of the *Cascade Mountains*, the *Olympic Mountains*, *Elliot Bay* and

Lake Washington are worth the effort. Your **PowerHike** of **Downtown Seattle** will

be unforgettable.

9

BAINBRIDGE ISLAND
BLOEDEL RESERVE

- -

Washington State Ferry Terminal Pier 52

The Bloedel Reserve

Winslow

Waterfront Park

TIME All day | **DISTANCE** 2 miles The Bloedel Reserve
1 mile around town

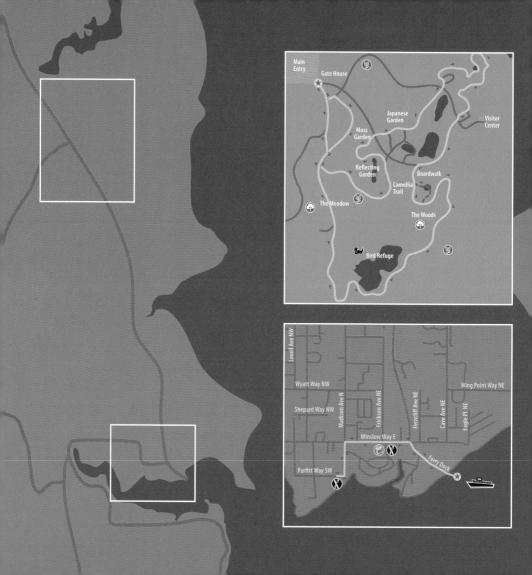

Map 1 (Garden)

Main Entry
Gate House
Japanese Garden
Moss Garden
Visitor Center
Reflecting Garden
Boardwalk
Camellia Trail
The Meadow
The Woods
Bird Refuge

Map 2 (Town)

Lovell Ave NW
Wyatt Way NW
Shepard Way NW
Madison Ave N
Erickson Ave NE
Ferncliff Ave NE
Cave Ave NE
Eagle Pl NE
Wing Point Way NE
Winslow Way E
Parfitt Way SW
Ferry Dock

A visit to ***The Bloedel Reserve*** on ***Bainbridge Island*** is an experience not to

be missed on a trip to ***Seattle***. This ***PowerHike*** takes us on two hours of absolute

delight wandering the paths of this spectacular horticultural paradise. Covering

150 acres, ***The Bloedel Reserve*** was once the estate of the Bloedel family,

prominent in the northwest lumber industry. Prentice Bloedel was a conservationist with great interest in renewable resources. His dream was for the gardens to maintain the tranquility of the estate, and he had the help of prominent landscape architects such as Thomas Church and Fujitaro Kubota to design it. *The Bloedel Reserve* can be explored on your own or through guided group tours. There is an amazing educational program with lectures, summer concerts, Christmas concerts, and a garden party.

The Bloedel Reserve is located on **Bainbridge Island**, reachable by ferry boat from downtown **Seattle. Bainbridge Island** was originally an

industrial hub for shipbuilding and logging. In recent years it has become a woodsy

suburb of **Seattle.** *Fort Ward State Park* is also located on **Bainbridge Island**. It is

densely forested and offers terrific views. The ferry boat ride takes 35 minutes and the vistas of the *Seattle* skyline and *Puget Sound* are spectacular. The ferry boat is a car ferry so you can go by car, bicycle or on foot. When you arrive at *Eagle Harbor*, there is a taxi or

bus available to reach *The Bloedel Reserve*, if you do not have a car. It is a short

15 minute drive through forested country roads. Upon reaching the *Gate House*, you can either meet your guide (make a reservation in advance) or obtain a map for your self-guided tour. Walk first through the tall grass of the *West Meadow*, once inhabited by sheep. Follow the trail towards the woods, where you will see many native northwest trees such as cedar, hemlock and Douglas fir. Continue on the

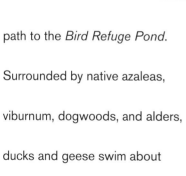

path to the *Bird Refuge Pond*.

Surrounded by native azaleas,

viburnum, dogwoods, and alders,

ducks and geese swim about

the pond. They live here year-round, but many migratory birds winter here and pass through. There is even a new resident beaver. Walk through *The Woods,* a native Northwest forest filled with fir and cedar, to the *Trestle Bridge.*

Gaze down at the stream as you cross the bridge, continuing on to the *Boardwalk,*

which allows you to walk through the wetlands without disturbing the plants. As you come out of the deep woods and wetlands, you encounter the beautiful formally

landscaped lakes and the residence beyond. Surrounded by willows and towering

elms on each side, it is an inspiring sight. This French country home is now the visitor

center and has a library with an astounding collection of horticultural and botanical

books. Beyond are spectacular views of **Puget Sound** and *Port Madison Bay*. Leave

the visitor center for the waterfall and the stunning *Rhododendron Glen*. Follow

the trail to the right into the *Birch Garden,* filled with birch trees, rhododendrons,

Japanese maples, hydrangeas, and an

amazingly large cyclamen garden. Follow

the *Orchid Trail* to the *Japanese Garden*,

a profusion of Japanese maples and the

stone and sand of the *Zen Garden*. Beyond

is the *Moss Garden*, quiet, serene, lush, and

marvelous. At the yew hedge enclosed *Reflection Pool*, you return to English landscaping, serenity, and solitude. Follow the *Camellia Trail* among giant vivid camellias to return to the *Meadow*. This inspired creation of natural wooded areas and landscaped gardens is a very special **PowerHike**. Open Wednesday through Sunday.

Follow the visit with a stop in *Winslow* for some refreshment. If you are not visiting

The Bloedel Reserve, *Winslow* is a short, 15 minute walk from the ferry landing at *Eagle Harbor*. The main street, *Winslow Way East*, is only a few blocks long, with interesting cafés, shops, and an

excellent bookstore, *Eagle Harbor Book Co.* Turn left at the church to walk down to *Waterfront Park*. The *Harbor Pub* is on the waterfront, a delightful spot to relax and enjoy the view of the sailboats and **Seattle** across the water. The end of this

PowerHike is a relaxing ferry boat ride back to the *Seattle* waterfront, a perfect time

to appreciate the breathtaking views and the glorious gardens seen today.

10

QUEEN ANNE

- - - - - - - - - - - - - - -

TIME 3–4 hours | **DISTANCE** 3.5 miles
plus all of the stairways explored

W McGraw St

Queen Anne Ave N

W Galer St

7th Ave W

Parson
Garden

W Highland Dr

Betty Bowen
Viewpoint

Queen Anne Ave N

Kerry Park

W Prospect St

The *Queen Anne* neighborhood in *Seattle* has historical elegance and spectacular views. Close to downtown and located on the city's highest hill, this lovely neighborhood flourished in the early 1900s, when cable cars carried people to the top of the hill. Today it is a popular destination for fun shops and cafés.

The early *Seattle* settlers built impressive homes to reflect their financial status and acquired wealth in *Queen Anne*, which was named for the style of Victorian architecture in fashion in the 1880s and 1890s.

The amazing turrets, bow windows, and gabled roofs are emblematic of the Gilded Age in America. Many homes on these beautiful tree lined streets in the *Queen Anne* neighborhood are historic landmarks, and wandering the crown, or upper part, of *Queen Anne* is a pleasure you will not want to miss. This

neighborhood is also known for its many stairways, each with its own history and captivating story. There is the Boston Street Haunted Stair, the Comstock Grand Dame, and the Galer Crown, to name a few. A map of these stairways is available from the Queen Anne Historical Society and well worth having with you, as it is filled with fascinating stories about this unique aspect of **Seattle**. What great fun to walk up and down these many historic stairways!

Queen Anne is located just above the **Seattle Center** and the **Space Needle**. It is the highest hill in central

Seattle, almost 500 feet, and the views of the city and *Puget Sound* are spectacular. The city's television and radio antennas are here. We start the *PowerHike* at the corner of *Queen Anne Avenue* and *West Highland Street*, known as the *Counterbalance*. In the early 20th century, cable cars were replaced by electric cars to get up steep *Queen Anne Avenue* from downtown to the crown of the hill, and a system of balances and weights was put in to help the cars up and down the hill. Hence the name *Counterbalance*. The famous house where the *Counterbalance* was located is on the corner. Today, you can get there on foot, by car, or by Seattle's convenient bus system. (*From downtown Seattle, several buses go to Queen Anne, such as MT 1,*

MT 13, and MT 15, and they run frequently.)

Walk west on *West Highland Street*. Note the

gabled house on the corner at *1 West Highland*

Street. Built by Whitney Treat for his family

and fourteen servants, it is now a private apartment

building. Continue down the street to *Kerry Park*,

admiring the lovely and gracious homes and the historic

Ballard Mansion as you walk. *Kerry Park* offers

an incredible view of the **Seattle** skyline and

is on the corner of *West Highland Street* and

2nd Avenue West. You can see *Elliott Bay, Alki,*

the Waterfront, Seattle Center and the *Space*

Needle –

through a

telescope if you wish. As you look out to the right,

there are grain elevators at the water's edge, and

up the hill from them is the charming *Magnolia*

neighborhood. *Changing Form*, the sculpture, is

a popular park attraction. On either side of *Kerry*

Park is one of the famous *Queen Anne* stairways. Take one down to *Prospect Avenue* and turn right walking to the next staircase. Walk up the stairs, returning to *West Highland Street*. Go left and continue walking down *West Highland Street.*

At *6th Avenue West,* another staircase goes up the hill to *West*

Comstock Street. At *West Highland Street* and *7th Avenue West* is the small,

charming *Parsons Garden Park*. Serene and peaceful with beautiful flowers, this park is a popular spot for weddings. Wander through and enjoy the beautiful azaleas and rhododendrons. Directly across the street is yet another vista point,

Betty Bowen Viewpoint, with decorated mosaics in the cement created by local artists and stairways leading down the hill. Follow the sidewalk curving to the right and bordered by street lamps as it becomes *7th Avenue*

West. Walk on towards *West Galer Street* and you will

see more of the stairways climbing up and down the hills.

At *West Galer Street,* climb the stone steps and walk

through the neighborhood of typical Queen Anne homes.

Continue on *West Galer*

Street, passing the West

Queen Anne Elementary

School, built in 1896,

now condominiums, and

turn left onto *Queen*

Anne Avenue North. You

are entering the delightful neighborhood shopping

and café district. Across the street is *5 Spot*, a

unique diner serving cuisine from across the country.

Its menus and décor change four times a year as

the food showcases US history and culture. It is a

distinctive, local venue, worth a visit. You will love

the iced tea served in jelly jars! Open for breakfast

through midnight seven days a week, what a fun and

educational spot! After a delightful meal, wander up the street as far as *West McGraw Street*, enjoying

the interesting local shops, cafés, bistros, *The Teacup*, and *Chocolopolis*. Check

out *Queen Anne Books*, well known in the neighborhood and another location to find the stairway map. After this adventuresome **PowerHike**, enjoy a meal, coffee, or stop at the local bakery or ice cream shop. **Queen Anne** is a neighborhood to enjoy, and you will want to take it all in.

11

ALKI BEACH

- -

Elliott Bay Water Taxi

Seacrest Marina

Salty's

Hamilton Viewpoint Park

Alki Village

Alki Beach Park

Alki Statue Of Liberty

Pioneer Monument

Log House Museum

Alki Point Lighthouse

TIME All day | **DISTANCE** 5 miles

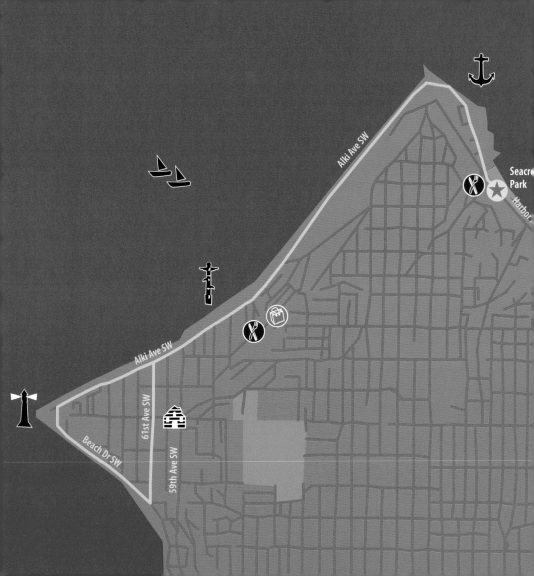

Alki Ave SW

Seacr
Park

Harbor

Beach Dr SW

61st Ave SW

59th Ave SW

With dazzling views of the *Seattle* skyline, *Elliott Bay*, and the surrounding *Olympic Mountains*, **Alki Beach** is a popular and enjoyable spot to visit. The beachfront is spectacular in its setting and its vistas and on a sunny day it is breathtaking. **Alki Beach** is the site where the Denny Party, a group of explorers, first landed in 1851, hoping to build a settlement there as a base for shipping lumber. It turned out that part of *Elliott Bay* was too shallow

for cargo ships, so they found deeper water across the bay on the shores of the future location of the city of **Seattle**. Today **Alki** is known as **West Seattle**, and is a delightful residential and recreation location. It is a short, inexpensive water taxi trip

from Pier 55 at the waterfront to *Seacrest Dock* at *Alki Point* in **Alki**. The boat ride

is a fun excursion across *Elliott Bay*, and the views of **Seattle** are stunning, as are

the views of the *Olympic Mountains*, the *Cascade Mountains*, *Vaschon Island*, and

Bainbridge Island. There are many cafés and restaurants at **Alki Beach**, and the

PowerHiking offers majestic northwest scenery.

This *PowerHike* starts at Pier 55 on the waterfront. Board the *Elliott Bay Water*

Taxi to *Seacrest Park Marina.* The water taxi runs from May through the beginning

of September; the fare is $3 one way, the ride is 12 minutes, and the vistas are the finest to be seen anywhere.

When you disembark, to your

left on the point is *Salty's,* a

well known and award winning

restaurant. Even though it is a

tourist magnet, it is worth a visit for refreshment or a meal. The interior décor is

kitschy, the views from the deck unbeatable, and it is one of **Seattle's** best known

waterfront restaurants. There is also a smaller café and a kayak rental at the Marina,

so you have some places to visit

either on your arrival or before you

catch the water taxi back to *Seattle*.

Plan your *PowerHiking* day to

include watching

the sunset from

Salty's, and

catching the last

boat back. The

lights flickering

on along the *Seattle*

skyline, highlighted

by the *Space Needle*, is a truly stunning sight.

To the right of the dock where you disembark the water taxi, a path meanders along the water and beach into the village of **Alki.** It is shared by walkers, runners, dog walkers, skaters, and everyone

else. You pass *Hamilton Viewpoint Park* and, as you continue, notice the many enhancements made by the Seattle Parks and Recreation and the local Historical Society. At *Luna Park* there was once an amusement park, complete with Ferris wheel. Ferry boats brought turn-of-the-century **Seattle** families for the day. An old

anchor marks the spot and recalls
the days of the sailing ships. Today
the maritime activity on *Elliott
Bay* is quite busy with tug boats,
freighters, container ships, ferry
boats, and the many pleasure

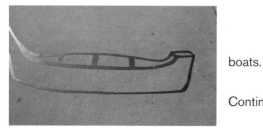

boats.

Continue along the beach path towards

the village. Across the road there
are many newly built condominiums
interspersed with a few remaining
vintage beach houses. There is an

old bathhouse that has been renovated and is now the Alki Bathhouse Art Studio.

Barbeque pits and picnic tables are available, and the feeling is reminiscent of a

Southern California beach. There are bikes, scooters, kayaks, surf gear, surrey bikes and all forms of water gear for rent. Most of all there is fun. *Alki Beach* is synonymous with fun, so enjoy! On a sunny day,

Alki Beach Park is the place to be.

In the small commercial block of the village are the

surf and swim shops, cafés, open air

restaurants, an ice cream store, and coffee shops

abound. Continue along the beach walk on *Alki*

Avenue Southwest to a tiny replica of the *Statue*

of Liberty. One block up from the beach on *61st*

Avenue Southwest is the *Log House Museum*, a

history museum open Thursday through Sunday and run by the Southwest Seattle Historical Society. It contains objects and photos of old *West Seattle* and

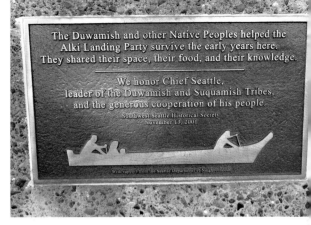

there is a gift shop behind the museum. Back on the beach

walk is the monument dedicated to the founders of **Seattle**,

Pioneer Monument. As you walk, turn left onto *Beach Drive*

Southwest and you will see the sign for our destination, the *Alki Point Lighthouse.* It is open on week ends and summer holidays from noon to 4PM and maintained by the Coast Guard. Return to *Alki Avenue Southwest* and the beach walk, and take time to sit on one of the many benches and enjoy the astounding scenery. Visit one of the chic local eateries such as *Cactus, Alki Bakery,* or *Spud's* and enjoy a beachfront meal, or return to *Seacrest Marina Park* and indulge in some much deserved rest and refreshment at *Salty's* while taking

in the spectacular vistas before you. The water taxi ride back to *Seattle* awaits you.

Note: There are buses that run along Alki Beach SW as well as a free beach transit.

12 SEWARD PARK

- -

Lake Washington

Coleman Park

Ampitheater

Lacey V. Murrow Bridge

Mercer Island

Mount Rainier

Andrews Bay Swimming Beaches

Artist Studio

TIME 3–4 hours | **DISTANCE** 2 miles/Lake Washington Blvd. S
2.4 miles/Seward Park

Coleman Park

LAKE WASHINGTON

Lake Washington Blvd S

ANDREWS
BAY

Seward Park

Lake Washington Blvd S

Seward Park
Clay Studio

Located on the shores of **Lake Washington**, **Seward Park** is a jewel in the **Seattle** park system and a fascinating *PowerHike*. The land on *Bailey Peninsula* was purchased by the city in 1910, and trails and picnic areas were built. It was named after William H. Seward, secretary of state under President Lincoln and the man responsible for the purchase of Alaska. The Yukon expansion and rush for gold followed, and the boom of the city of **Seattle** began. **Seward Park** is a 300 acre peninsula extending out into the lake, and the views are glorious – from downtown **Seattle** to *Mount Rainier*. There are hiking trails, beaches, picnic areas, an art studio, and even an amphitheater. If your visit is during the summer, you can

enjoy the Shakespeare in the Park series, which takes place in the lovely wooded amphitheater. *Seward Park* is distinctively wooded with many native trees, such as Douglas fir, big leaf maple and madrona. The older native forest is the largest in the city. It is also home to beavers, raccoons, mice, woodpeckers, owls, and bald eagles. Along the shores you will find ducks, grebes, kingfishers, and even great blue herons. The park was originally designed by the Olmstead Brothers.

We include a walk along the shores of *Lake Washington* in this *PowerHike,* and begin at *Coleman Park* on *Lake Washington*

Blvd. South at *Lake Park Drive.* Walk south on

Lake Washington Blvd. S., basking in the splendid

views of the lake and mountains to the left. If it is

springtime, the cherry trees are in bloom and are a

magnificent site. As you enter **Seward Park,** you

will see that it is filled with

picnic areas and trails to

explore. One trail goes up

over the top of the peninsula

to the amphitheater. Spend

as much time as you would

like exploring and enjoying

the beauty of the

forest. This *PowerHike*

follows the main trail,

which loops around

the water's edge, a

distance of 2.4 miles,

and is the most picturesque, offering the best lake and mountain vistas. It is a

thoroughly entrancing walk with views of the city and *Mount Rainier* in the distance.

At the farthest point out in the lake you will have an excellent view of *Mercer Island*.

Connected to the mainland by the *Lacey V. Murrow Bridge, Mercer Island* is an

enclave of narrow winding streets and charming homes terraced down the hillsides

to the water. It is one of the most beautiful residential neighborhoods in ***Seattle.***

Rounding the end of the peninsula you pass rocky beaches as you approach

Andrews Bay and the best swimming beaches in the park. At the end of the trail is

the artist studio. It is a clay studio that was once a bath house for the beach.

At this point you can venture on to some of the other trails in the park to further

explore the beauty of **Seward Park**, but the **PowerHike** turns right at *Lake*

Washington Blvd. South and returns to *Coleman Park*.

13 KIRKLAND

- - - - - - - - - - - - -

TIME 4 hours | **DISTANCE** 3 miles

All day if partaking in water activities

LAKE WASHINGTON

Central Way

Park

Main

Kirkland Ave

Marina Park

Lake St S

David E.
Brink Park

Marsh Park

Lake Washington Blvd NE

Houghton
Beach Park

Carillon Point
Woodmark Hotel

On the east side of **Lake Washington**

is the suburb of **Kirkland**. With a

picturesque downtown waterfront, the

city offers chic restaurants with sparkling

views, beautifully groomed parks,

beaches, art galleries, a performing arts

center, boating activities, and water

sports. It has become a weekend destination as well as

a very desirable residential community. There is public

access to **Lake Washington** for recreation and dramatic

views of the **Seattle** skyline. The shopping streets are

charming and fun to explore. *Kirkland Marina Park*

stretches along the lakeshore downtown and provides a beautiful beach area, docks

for the many pleasure boats, and a wonderful gathering spot for the community. It

is a pretty spot for a picnic, to take a swim or to enjoy the farmers' market in the

summertime. There is no ferry to **Kirkland** from **Seattle**, so you must drive across the *Evergreen Point Floating Bridge*, take a bus (MT251 from 4th Avenue) or go by taxi (Eastside for Hire.) There is the

Argosy Ferry Cruise around the lake – including waterside vistas of the beautiful

residential areas – a must when visiting **Kirkland**. This **PowerHike** follows the

trail that meanders along the shores of **Lake Washington** connecting the lakeside

parks, passing upscale condominiums, hotels, and restaurants, and exploring the

shops and galleries in the small commercial village. Be sure to time your *PowerHike* so that you can take one of Argosy Cruises around the lake (800-642-7816, www.argosycruises.

com). A cruise lasts about an hour and a half, and the last cruise is mid-afternoon.

There are also private boats that can be chartered for lake excursions and water

adventures (www.seattlewatersports.com).

Start this *PowerHike* later in the morning or in the afternoon to experience a

beautiful *Seattle* sunset from the shores of *Lake Washington*. Once in *Kirkland*,

explore *Marina Park*, location of the summer farmers' market, and walk along the

boat docks admiring the many

beautiful pleasure craft. These are

year round boat docks available to

rent for incoming craft. Take a swim

in the lake, indulge in waterskiing

or tubing, or just stick your toes

in at water's edge. *Marina Park* has a lovely pavilion, a grassy picnic area, and

designated fishing areas – a superb spot to spend the afternoon. From the *Marina*

take *Kirkland Avenue* to *Lake Street South,* turn left to *Park Lane* and turn right for

some gallery and

antique browsing.

Walk left on *Main*

Street to *Central*

as far as *Market,*

visiting the specialty

shops on your way back to *Lake Street South*. Turn right and

walk along *Lake Street*

South window shopping

and snooping. Once past the shops, you

will see the well-groomed condominiums

that line *Lake Street South*. After passing

Anthony's (famous for its seafood and spectacular views) follow *Lake Street South* to *David E. Brink Park*, with a Native American sculpture, ***The Water Bearers***. Next, take the pathway to the shore for an unobstructed view of the ***Seattle*** skyline. At *Marsh Park*, *Lake Street South* becomes *Lake Washington Blvd. NE*. A highlight

of the park is its lifelike

Leapfrog sculpture. In

the height of summer,

people come to the

public parks and beaches

to swim in **Lake Washington**

and enjoy waterskiing and

other boating activities. A chic

eatery is the *Beach House*

Bar & Grill, which you will find

just before reaching *Houghton*

Beach Park. It is popular so

reservations are recommended. A play area, boat dock, and restrooms are to be found in *Houghton Beach Park*. Just beyond is another trendy site, the luxury hotel and marina at *One Carillon Point*. Walk on the pathway down to a sculpture garden, and take the bridge over Carillon Creek. After you reach the marina, go up the stairway into the stylish *Woodmark Hotel* and its shops.

Before retracing you steps back to *Marina Park*, choose one of the picturesque restaurants you have walked by to relax and enjoy the majestic views of **Lake Washington** and the **Seattle** skyline while indulging in a fine meal. It will be difficult to find a more beautiful scenic location than the shores of **Lake Washington**. While particularly spectacular at dusk and sunset, the vistas are truly remarkable at any time of day.

14

LAKE UNION

- - - - - - - - - - - - - -

TIME 3 hours | **DISTANCE** 3 miles

LAKE UNION

Kenmore
Air Harbor

South
Lake Union
Park

Center for
Wooden
Boats

Historic Ships Wharf
Indian Canoe Center

Fairview Ave N

Westlake Ave

Westlake Ave 6th Ave

5th Ave

Close to downtown *Seattle*, *Lake Union* and the newly renovated *South Lake Union Park* are unique in an urban setting. Celebrating the maritime heritage of the area, as well as the industrial history, it is a locale where you can experience the abounding maritime culture of the city of *Seattle*, from the Duwamish Indians to the first Boeing Airplane hangar built in 1915. There are sailing classes, boat rentals, historic boats, pleasure boats, kayaks, sea planes, the *Center for Wooden Boats*, the *Historic Ships Wharf*, and wildlife. The recently opened park is a result of unending effort by Microsoft co-founder, Paul Allen. Through his energy and donations, the

park has become a reality and a treasure to the neighborhood. A pathway around the lake takes you past the many enticing entertainment and eating establishments, and also many fabulous expensive yachts. New office buildings, condos and apartments

have been built, and the area is quickly becoming a fun place to live instead of the former industrial area rarely frequented by tourists or *Seattle* natives. There are even floating homes around the lake's shores. In fact, one was featured in the film *Sleepless In Seattle* as the home of the character played by Tom Hanks. There is shopping, anchored by Whole Foods Market, hotels, good food, lively entertainment, and easy transportation to and from the city center. The *South Lake Union Streetcar* brings you directly from downtown to the park's edge.

We start this **PowerHike** in downtown *Seattle* at the *Westlake Center* (*Westlake Avenue* between *5th* and *6th* Avenues) and board the *South Lake Union Streetcar*. This relatively recently constructed streetcar line links the neighborhood with downtown and approximately follows *Seattle's* first railroad path.

The cars are clean and colorful, and the 2.6 mile line is an easy

and efficient way to navigate the area. The adult fare is $2.50 and

there are fare boxes for ticket purchase. It runs every 15 minutes

daily between the corner of *Westlake* and *Olive*, downtown, and

Ward and *Fairview* in *South Lake Union*.

Get off the street car in *South Lake Union* across the street from

the Fred Hutchinson Cancer Research Center on *Fairview Avenue North* at *Ward*

Street. Known as one of *Seattle's* most walkable neighborhoods, it has much to see

and many historical buildings and landmarks. However, we save the neighborhood

walk for another time, and explore the lake and park on this *PowerHike*. At the north

end of the lake in the distance you can see *Gas Works Park*, an area of greenery surrounding large industrial structures no longer in use. It is a popular site for water

sports, picnics, and community events. Cross to the *Fairview Walkway* on the

water and *South Lake Union Park* at the southern end of the lake. There you will

 find green space, picnic areas, trees, an enormous

interactive fountain, a model boat pond, boat rentals,

and moorings for many luxury yachts. It is very popular

in this growing neighborhood. The *Historic Ships*

Wharf is next to the Naval Reserve Center (soon to be

the Museum of History and Industry), where you can see the steamer *Virginia V.*, the

lightship *Swiftsure*, the tugboat *Arthur Foss*, and the fireship *Duwamish*, along with

many historical vessels that visit the wharf. The *Northwest Native Canoe Center* is

nearby. The *Chesiahud Loop* is a path around the lake that will be 6 miles in length designed for bicycles and walking and beautifully landscaped.

It would be a lovely way to spend the day *PowerHiking*

around *Lake Union* but we do a shorter *PowerHike* at the

southern end of the lake. At the streetcar stop, walk across to

the *Fairview Walkway* along the water, turning left and passing

restaurants, boat rentals, and people enjoying the water and

the out of doors. The *Indian Canoe Center* is on the left. Visit

the canoes on the way along the water to the *Historic Ships*

Wharf and

the *Center*

for *Wooden*

Boats. You

The Steamship Virginia V

The Steam Ship *Virginia V* was built in 1922 to carry freight and passengers from Vashon Island to Seattle and Tacoma. Once one of over 300 ships of her type, she is the last operating vessel from the famous Puget Sound "Mosquito Fleet."

Now a National Historic Landmark Vessel, the *Virginia V* continues her mission of providing a unique view into the "golden age of steam."

The Center for WOODEN BOATS

can board the ships and then continue over the bridge and through *South Lake Union Park*. Operated by Seattle Parks and Recreation, it is 12 acres of green space with water access. Continue through the park and north to *Kenmore Air Harbor*, home to a large, well-respected fleet of seaplanes. There are regularly scheduled flights for sightseeing or connecting to other airports. At this point, you can continue on to complete the 6 mile loop of the lake or retrace your steps to one of the fine waterfront restaurants passed earlier for a meal on the water's edge. With a wide array of eateries, you will be sure to find a waterside spot to please. Return to the streetcar and downtown to the many delights of the *Westlake Center* locale.